Great Americans

Harriet Tubman

Monica L. Rausch

Reading consultant: Susan Nations, M.Ed., author/literacy coach/
consultant in literacy development

Please visit our web site at: www.garethstevens.com
For a free color catalog describing Weekly Reader® Early Learning Library's list
of high-quality books, call 1-877-445-5824 (USA) or 1-800-387-3178 (Canada).
Weekly Reader® Early Learning Library's fax: (414) 336-0164.

Library of Congress Cataloging-in-Publication Data

Rausch, Monica.
    Harriet Tubman / by Monica L. Rausch.
      p. cm. — (Great Americans)
    Includes bibliographical references and index.
    ISBN-13: 978-0-8368-7686-4 (lib. bdg.)
    ISBN-13: 978-0-8368-7693-2 (softcover)
      1. Tubman, Harriet, 1820?-1913—Juvenile literature.   2. African American women—
Biography—Juvenile literature.   3. African Americans—Biography—Juvenile literature.
4. Slaves—United States—Biography—Juvenile literature.
5. Underground railroad—Juvenile literature. I. Title.
    E444.T82R38   2007
    973.7'115092—dc22
    [B]   2006032591

This edition first published in 2007 by
Weekly Reader® Early Learning Library
A Member of the WRC Media Family of Companies
330 West Olive Street, Suite 100
Milwaukee, WI 53212 USA

Copyright © 2007 by Weekly Reader® Early Learning Library

Managing editor: Valerie J. Weber
Art direction: Tammy West
Cover design and page layout: Charlie Dahl
Picture research: Sabrina Crewe
Production: Jessica Yanke and Robert Kraus

Picture credits: Cover, title page, pp. 6, 8, 10, 12 © North Wind Picture Archives; pp. 5, 7, 13, 16
© The Granger Collection, New York; p. 9 Charlie Dahl/© Weekly Reader Early Learning Library;
p. 14 © Louie Psihoyos/CORBIS; pp. 17, 20 Library of Congress; p. 18 © Bettmann/CORBIS;
p. 21 © AP Images

Printed in the United States of America

1 2 3 4 5 6 7 8 9 10 10 09 08 07 06

Table of Contents

Cover and title page: Harriet Tubman risked her life to rescue men, women, and children from slavery.

Chapter 1

Escaping to Freedom

Every footstep of the escaping **slaves** echoed loudly in the night. Their leader, Harriet Tubman, knew their route well, but even she was careful. At any minute, slave hunters could catch the group. They would be taken back to **slavery**. They would be beaten for running away and be forced to work for no pay.

Tubman knew these risks, but she was willing to take them. She had known life as a slave herself and had escaped from slavery. Once she was free, Tubman helped others. During her lifetime, Tubman helped more than three hundred slaves escape to freedom.

Even after slavery ended, Tubman worked hard to help African Americans and women. She helped start schools like this one for freed slaves.

Slaves worked in the fields and houses of many farms in the southern United States. Here, slaves are picking cotton.

We do not know much about Harriet Tubman's early life. She was born between 1820 and 1825 on a **plantation** in Bucktown, Maryland. Her mother, Harriet Green, and her father, Benjamin Ross, were slaves. They named her Araminta Ross.

When Tubman was five or six years old, her owner sent her to work at a neighbor's house. There, she helped care for the neighbor's baby. If the baby cried at night and woke its mother, the mother whipped Tubman.

Like Tubman, this young slave girl took care of children.

Overseers, like the one on horseback here, completely controlled slaves on many plantations. Some overseers were kind, while others were cruel.

When Tubman was about twelve, she went to the store one day to buy some food for the plantation's cook. At the store, a slave **overseer** was trying to punish another slave. As the slave ran out of the store, Tubman bravely stood in the doorway to stop the overseer from following him.

The angry overseer threw a heavy metal weight at the running slave. The weight did not hit the slave — it hit Tubman instead. Tubman was badly hurt.

North Wind Picture Archives

In 1844, Tubman met and married a free African American man named John Tubman. Five years later, Harriet's owner died. She thought her new owner might sell her. Harriet, however, did not want to be sold or be a slave any longer.

At that time, the states in the northern United States did not allow slavery. Tubman had to escape to the north to be free.

States and areas in orange on this map allowed people to have slaves. States and areas in blue did not allow slavery.

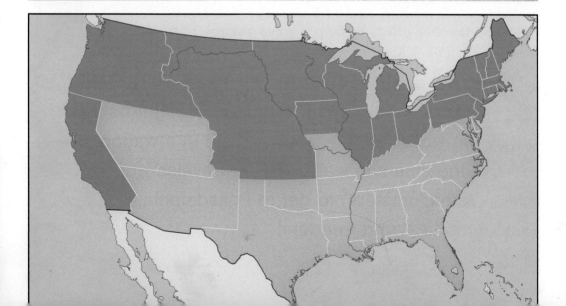

Abolitionists were people who believed that slaves should be free. Here, a teacher offers to help a slave escape to freedom.

In the fall of 1849, Tubman ran away. An **abolitionist** told her about some other people who might help her get to the North. Sometimes she hid in a wagon, but most of the time she walked. She traveled about 100 miles (160 kilometers) to get to Philadelphia, Pennsylvania — and freedom!

Chapter 2

Helping Other Slaves

The people who helped Tubman were part of the
Underground Railroad. The Underground Railroad
was not a real railroad with trains and train stations.
Instead, it was a secret group of people who helped
slaves escape.

Plantation owners paid slave hunters (like the two men with hats here) to look for escaped slaves. Some plantation owners wanted to give a $40,000 **reward** to anyone who could catch Tubman.

Tubman was happy to be free, but she wanted her family to be free, too. She stayed in Philadelphia for just one year. Then she risked her life and her freedom to go back to Maryland. She wanted to help her sister and her sister's children escape.

Over the next ten years, Tubman made more than nineteen trips to the South to help more than three hundred slaves escape to freedom. After 1850, she had to take the slaves even farther north. A new law said that any slave who escaped to the Northern states could be brought back to the South to be a slave again. Tubman knew that they would have to go to Canada to be free.

Tubman *(far left)* helped these slaves escape to Canada.

One man dug a tunnel between these two buildings in Wisconsin. Escaped slaves used the tunnel to get to the man's home, where his family hid them.

Tubman had many ways to hide the slaves during their escapes. They often traveled at night when it was harder for slave owners to find them. Sometimes they spoke to each other in songs. The songs had codes in them that told the slaves the safest ways to travel.

Chapter 3

Helping the Army

Leaders of states in the North and South started to argue more about what states could do. They also argued about slavery. People in the South believed that state governments should be very powerful. They also thought that they needed slavery to keep plantations running. In 1860, the Southern states decided to leave, or **secede** from, the United States.

The Northern states did not want the Southern states to secede. In 1861, the North and the South began fighting. The Civil War had begun!

During the Civil War, Tubman helped the North's army. She worked as a spy. She knew the land in the South, and she knew how to move in secret.

The South fired the first shots of the Civil War at Fort Sumter in South Carolina.

Tubman even sailed on a boat with the army during a raid on some plantations. The slaves on the plantations rushed to the army's boats during the raid. Tubman helped eight hundred slaves get on the boats and go north to freedom.

Tubman sailed on a boat like this one when she helped the Northern army.

Tubman also worked as a nurse during the war. She nursed soldiers and escaped slaves. She also helped the freed slaves find jobs.

These slaves escaped from Virginia in 1862. The Civil War ended in June 1865. The North won, and the Southern states were part of the United States again.

Chapter 4

Life in New York

During the war, John Tubman died. In 1869, Harriet Tubman married Nelson Davis, and they lived in Auburn, New York. Tubman helped start a school for African American children. She also gave speeches about giving women and African Americans the right to vote.

When she was about eighty years old, Tubman started building a special home for the elderly. In 1911, she became sick and moved into the home. Harriet Tubman died on March 10, 1913. She was over ninety years old.

Harriet Tubman sits in a chair outside her home for the elderly in 1911. Today, people can visit the Harriet Tubman Home in Auburn, New York.

At her burial, the U.S. Army honored Tubman for her work. A World War II ship also was named after this strong and brave woman, who spent her life helping African Americans.

This statue was made in honor of Harriet Tubman and other escaped slaves. It stands in Boston, Massachusetts. The city of Auburn, New York, also named a park in her memory. It is named Freedom Park.

Glossary

abolitionist — a person who did not believe people should be slaves and who worked to free slaves

codes — symbols or words used to hide the meaning of a speech or a song

elderly — people who are older or advanced in years

overseer — a person who managed or directed the work of slaves in the fields on plantations

plantation — a large area of land that is farmed

raid — a surprise attack by a small group of people

reward — an amount of money that is given for finding something lost

secede — separate from or leave

slavery — the practice of keeping slaves, people who are made to work without pay and not allowed to be free

slaves — people who are treated as property and are forced to work without pay

Underground Railroad — a web of safe routes, safe places to stay, and people who helped slaves escape to freedom

For More Information

Books

Escape North! The Story of Harriet Tubman. Step-Into-Reading Step 4 (series). Monica Kulling (Random House)

Harriet Tubman and the Freedom Train. Sharon Gayle (Aladdin).

Minty: A Story of Young Harriet Tubman. Alan Schroeder (Penguin Young Readers Group).

Websites

The Library of Congress: America's Story — Harriet Tubman
www.americaslibrary.gov/cgi-bin/page.cgi/aa/tubman
The life story of Harriet Tubman with a time line of major events in her life

Time for Kids: Harriet Tubman
www.timeforkids.com/TFK/specials/articles/0,6709,714579,00.html
Information and quizzes on Harriet Tubman

Index

About the Author

Monica L. Rausch has a master's degree in creative writing from the University of Wisconsin-Milwaukee, where she is currently teaching composition, literature, and creative writing. She likes to write fiction, but sticking to the facts is fun, too. Monica lives in Milwaukee near her six nieces and nephews, to whom she loves to read books.